EDGAR RICE BURROUGHS'
JOHN CARTER OF MARS

CHARACTER IDENTITY

NAME:

RACE:

TITLE:

TALENTS

CORE EQUIPMENT

WEAPON:	
BASE DAMAGE:	NOTES:

WEAPON:	
BASE DAMAGE:	NOTES:

WEAPON:	
BASE DAMAGE:	NOTES:

WEAPON:	
BASE DAMAGE:	NOTES:

FLAW

NOTES

CONCEPT:

ATTRIBUTES

		TOTAL	WORST
CUNNING	+ DARING		
	+ EMPATHY		
	+ MIGHT		
	+ PASSION		
USED FOR ALL ATTACKS, INSULTS AND THEFTS	+ REASON		
DARING	+ CUNNING		
	+ EMPATHY		
	+ MIGHT		
	+ PASSION		
USED WHEN AT RISK AND MOVEMENT IS IMPORTANT	+ REASON		
EMPATHY	+ CUNNING		
	+ DARING		
	+ MIGHT		
	+ PASSION		
USED TO UNDERSTAND OR HEAL ANOTHER	+ REASON		
MIGHT	+ CUNNING		
	+ DARING		
	+ EMPATHY		
	+ PASSION		
USED TO APPLY FORCE TO THE INANIMATE WORLD	+ REASON		
PASSION	+ CUNNING		
	+ DARING		
	+ EMPATHY		
	+ MIGHT		
USED FOR ATTEMPTS TO LEAD, LOVE OR ENTERTAIN	+ REASON		
REASON	+ CUNNING		
	+ DARING		
	+ EMPATHY		
	+ MIGHT		
USED FOR ACTIONS THAT USE THE MIND OR THE SENSES	+ PASSION		

STRESS AND AFFLICTIONS

CONFUSION — EFFECTS: EMPATHY & REASON

STRESS
CONFUSION:

AFFLICTION
MADNESS:

FEAR — EFFECTS: DARING & PASSION

STRESS
FEAR:

AFFLICTION
TRAUMA:

INJURY — EFFECTS: CUNNING & MIGHT

STRESS
INJURY:

AFFLICTION
WOUNDS:

LUCK

RENOWN

UNSPENT	SPENT	TOTAL

REPUTATION AND EFFECTS:

EXPERIENCE

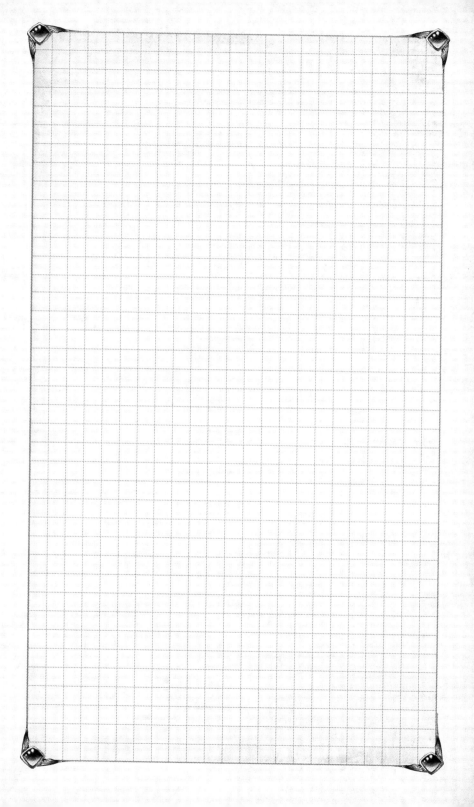

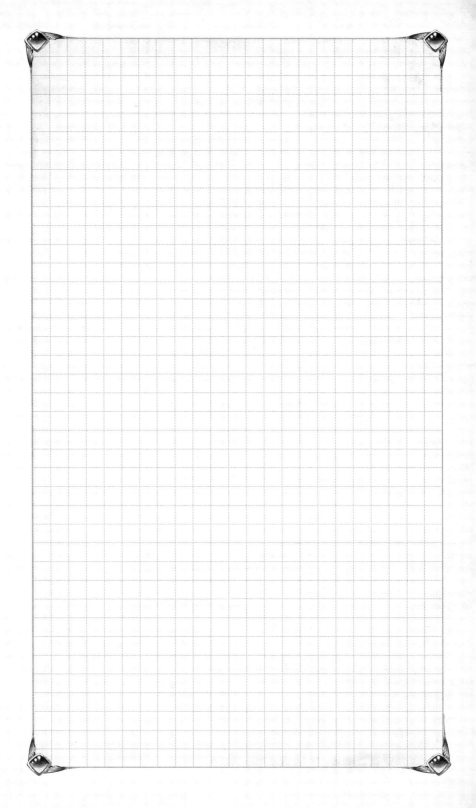

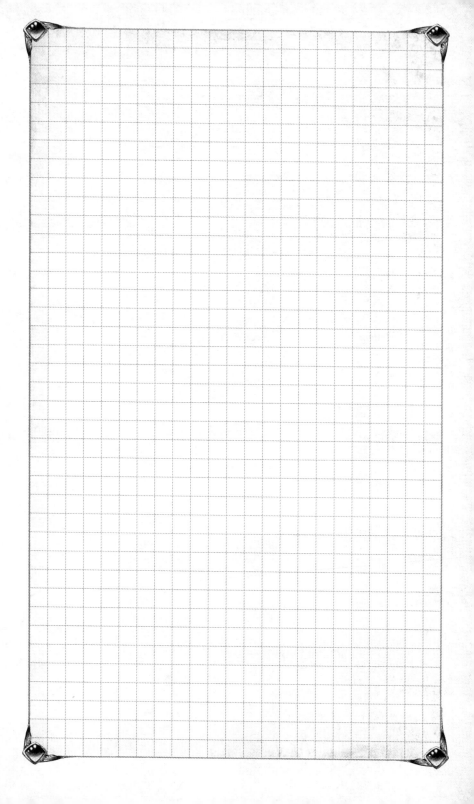

CHARACTER IDENTITY

NAME:

RACE:

TITLE:

TALENTS

CORE EQUIPMENT

WEAPON:	
BASE DAMAGE:	NOTES:

WEAPON:	
BASE DAMAGE:	NOTES:

WEAPON:	
BASE DAMAGE:	NOTES:

WEAPON:	
BASE DAMAGE:	NOTES:

FLAW

NOTES

CONCEPT:

ATTRIBUTES

		TOTAL	WORST
CUNNING	+ DARING		
	+ EMPATHY		
	+ MIGHT		
	+ PASSION		
USED FOR ALL ATTACKS, INSULTS AND THEFTS	+ REASON		
DARING	+ CUNNING		
	+ EMPATHY		
	+ MIGHT		
	+ PASSION		
USED WHEN AT RISK AND MOVEMENT IS IMPORTANT	+ REASON		
EMPATHY	+ CUNNING		
	+ DARING		
	+ MIGHT		
	+ PASSION		
USED TO UNDERSTAND OR HEAL ANOTHER	+ REASON		
MIGHT	+ CUNNING		
	+ DARING		
	+ EMPATHY		
	+ PASSION		
USED TO APPLY FORCE TO THE INANIMATE WORLD	+ REASON		
PASSION	+ CUNNING		
	+ DARING		
	+ EMPATHY		
	+ MIGHT		
USED FOR ATTEMPTS TO LEAD, LOVE OR ENTERTAIN	+ REASON		
REASON	+ CUNNING		
	+ DARING		
	+ EMPATHY		
	+ MIGHT		
USED FOR ACTIONS THAT USE THE MIND OR THE SENSES	+ PASSION		

STRESS AND AFFLICTIONS

CONFUSION EFFECTS: EMPATHY & REASON

STRESS
CONFUSION:

AFFLICTION
MADNESS:

FEAR EFFECTS: DARING & PASSION

STRESS
FEAR:

AFFLICTION
TRAUMA:

INJURY EFFECTS: CUNNING & MIGHT

STRESS
INJURY:

AFFLICTION
WOUNDS:

LUCK

RENOWN

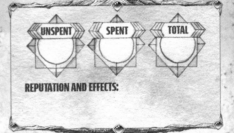

UNSPENT   SPENT   TOTAL

REPUTATION AND EFFECTS:

EXPERIENCE

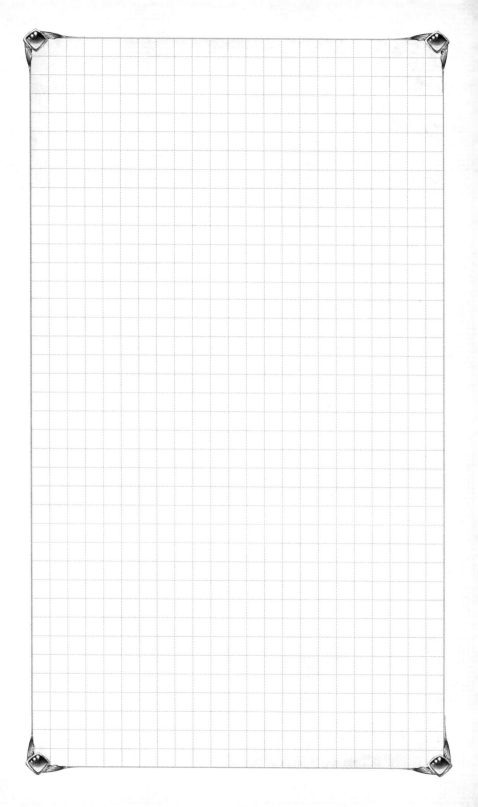

EDGAR RICE BURROUGHS'
JOHN CARTER OF MARS

CHARACTER IDENTITY

NAME:

RACE:

TITLE:

TALENTS

CORE EQUIPMENT

WEAPON:

BASE DAMAGE:	NOTES:

WEAPON:

BASE DAMAGE:	NOTES:

WEAPON:

BASE DAMAGE:	NOTES:

WEAPON:

BASE DAMAGE:	NOTES:

FLAW

NOTES

CONCEPT:

ATTRIBUTES

		TOTAL	WORST
CUNNING	+ DARING		
	+ EMPATHY		
	+ MIGHT		
	+ PASSION		
USED FOR ALL ATTACKS, INSULTS AND THEFTS	+ REASON		
DARING	+ CUNNING		
	+ EMPATHY		
	+ MIGHT		
	+ PASSION		
USED WHEN AT RISK AND MOVEMENT IS IMPORTANT	+ REASON		
EMPATHY	+ CUNNING		
	+ DARING		
	+ MIGHT		
	+ PASSION		
USED TO UNDERSTAND OR HEAL ANOTHER	+ REASON		
MIGHT	+ CUNNING		
	+ DARING		
	+ EMPATHY		
	+ PASSION		
USED TO APPLY FORCE TO THE INANIMATE WORLD	+ REASON		
PASSION	+ CUNNING		
	+ DARING		
	+ EMPATHY		
	+ MIGHT		
USED FOR ATTEMPTS TO LEAD, LOVE OR ENTERTAIN	+ REASON		
REASON	+ CUNNING		
	+ DARING		
	+ EMPATHY		
	+ MIGHT		
USED FOR ACTIONS THAT USE THE MIND OR THE SENSES	+ PASSION		

STRESS AND AFFLICTIONS

CONFUSION — EFFECTS: EMPATHY & REASON

STRESS
CONFUSION:

AFFLICTION
MADNESS:

FEAR — EFFECTS: DARING & PASSION

STRESS
FEAR:

AFFLICTION
TRAUMA:

INJURY — EFFECTS: CUNNING & MIGHT

STRESS
INJURY:

AFFLICTION
WOUNDS:

LUCK

RENOWN

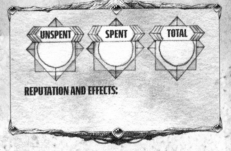

REPUTATION AND EFFECTS:

EXPERIENCE

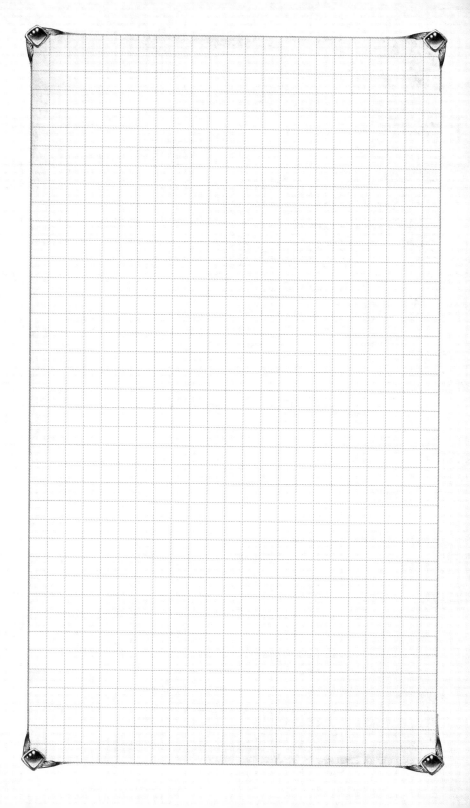

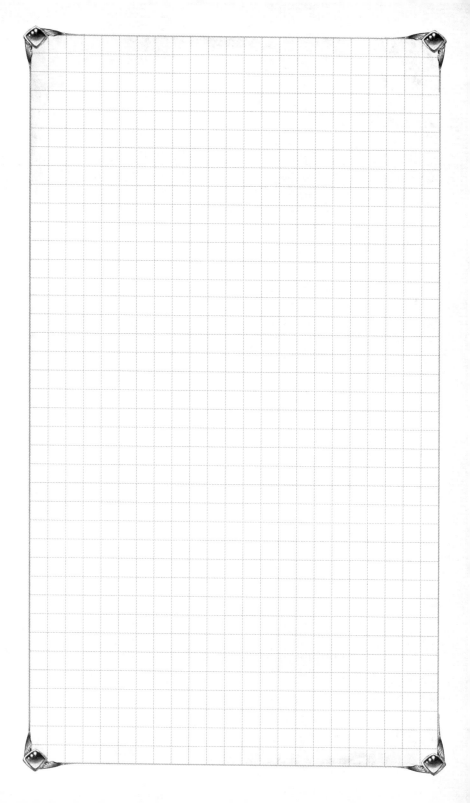

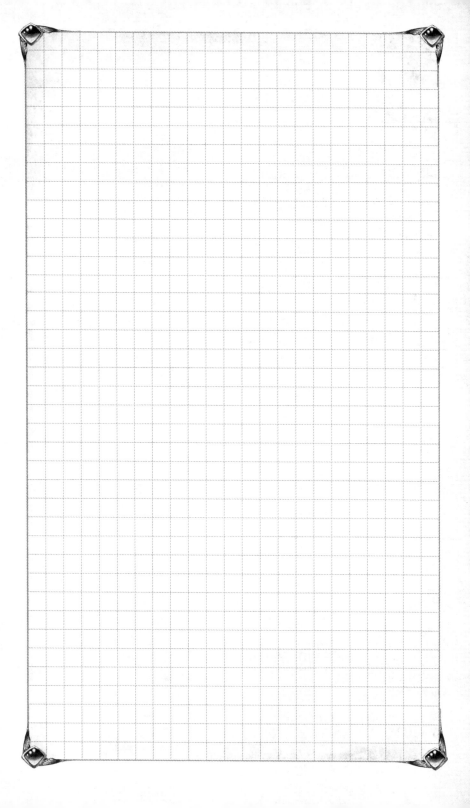

CHARACTER IDENTITY

NAME:

RACE:

TITLE:

TALENTS

CORE EQUIPMENT

WEAPON:

BASE DAMAGE: NOTES:

WEAPON:

BASE DAMAGE: NOTES:

WEAPON:

BASE DAMAGE: NOTES:

WEAPON:

BASE DAMAGE: NOTES:

FLAW

NOTES

CONCEPT:

ATTRIBUTES

		TOTAL	WORST
CUNNING	+ DARING		
	+ EMPATHY		
	+ MIGHT		
USED FOR ALL ATTACKS, INSULTS AND THEFTS	+ PASSION		
	+ REASON		
DARING	+ CUNNING		
	+ EMPATHY		
	+ MIGHT		
USED WHEN AT RISK AND MOVEMENT IS IMPORTANT	+ PASSION		
	+ REASON		
EMPATHY	+ CUNNING		
	+ DARING		
	+ MIGHT		
USED TO UNDERSTAND OR HEAL ANOTHER	+ PASSION		
	+ REASON		
MIGHT	+ CUNNING		
	+ DARING		
	+ EMPATHY		
USED TO APPLY FORCE TO THE INANIMATE WORLD	+ PASSION		
	+ REASON		
PASSION	+ CUNNING		
	+ DARING		
	+ EMPATHY		
USED FOR ATTEMPTS TO LEAD, LOVE OR ENTERTAIN	+ MIGHT		
	+ REASON		
REASON	+ CUNNING		
	+ DARING		
	+ EMPATHY		
USED FOR ACTIONS THAT USE THE MIND OR THE SENSES	+ MIGHT		
	+ PASSION		

STRESS AND AFFLICTIONS

CONFUSION — *EFFECTS: EMPATHY & REASON*

STRESS
CONFUSION:

AFFLICTION
MADNESS:

FEAR — *EFFECTS: DARING & PASSION*

STRESS
FEAR:

AFFLICTION
TRAUMA:

INJURY — *EFFECTS: CUNNING & MIGHT*

STRESS
INJURY:

AFFLICTION
WOUNDS:

LUCK

RENOWN

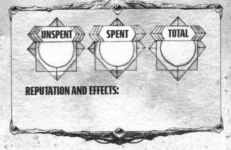

UNSPENT	SPENT	TOTAL

REPUTATION AND EFFECTS:

EXPERIENCE

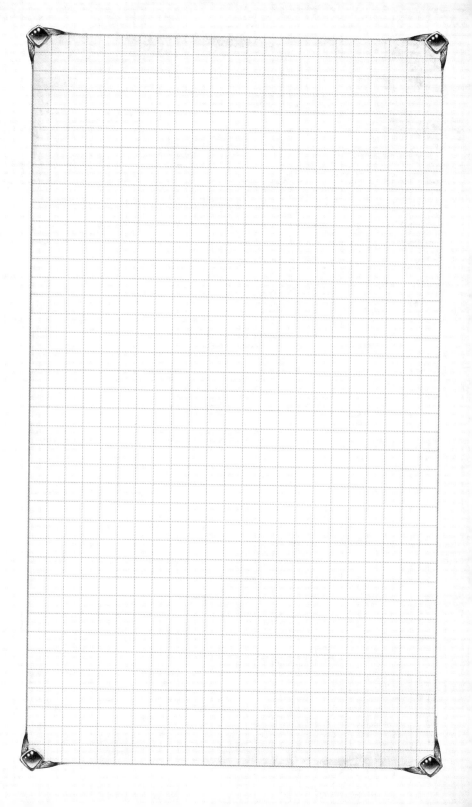

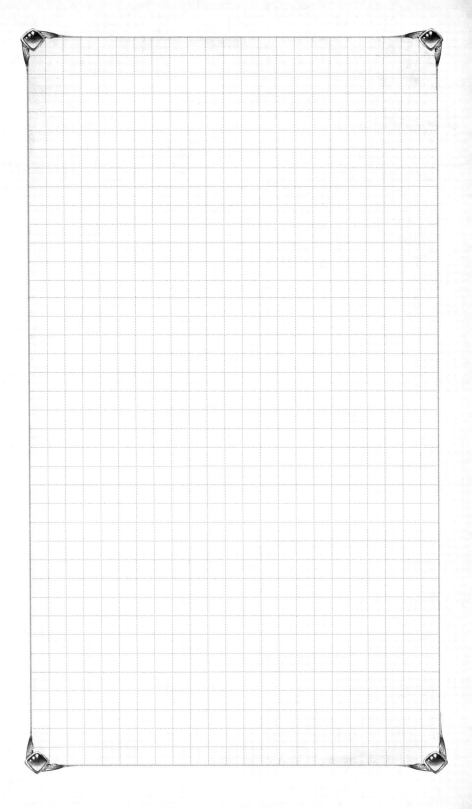

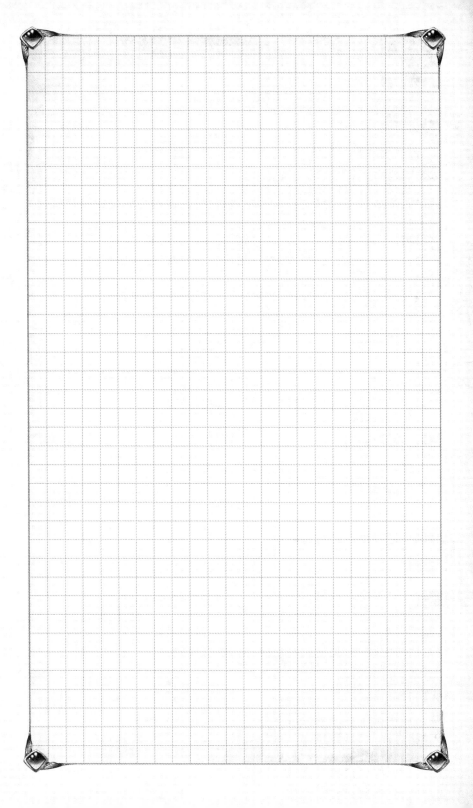

EDGAR RICE
BURROUGHS'
JOHN CARTER
OF MARS

CHARACTER IDENTITY

NAME:

RACE:

TITLE:

TALENTS

CORE EQUIPMENT

WEAPON:	
BASE DAMAGE:	NOTES:

WEAPON:	
BASE DAMAGE:	NOTES:

WEAPON:	
BASE DAMAGE:	NOTES:

WEAPON:	
BASE DAMAGE:	NOTES:

FLAW

NOTES

CONCEPT:

ATTRIBUTES

CUNNING
USED FOR ALL ATTACKS, INSULTS AND THEFTS

	TOTAL	WORST
+ DARING		
+ EMPATHY		
+ MIGHT		
+ PASSION		
+ REASON		

DARING
USED WHEN AT RISK AND MOVEMENT IS IMPORTANT

+ CUNNING		
+ EMPATHY		
+ MIGHT		
+ PASSION		
+ REASON		

EMPATHY
USED TO UNDERSTAND OR HEAL ANOTHER

+ CUNNING		
+ DARING		
+ MIGHT		
+ PASSION		
+ REASON		

MIGHT
USED TO APPLY FORCE TO THE INANIMATE WORLD

+ CUNNING		
+ DARING		
+ EMPATHY		
+ PASSION		
+ REASON		

PASSION
USED FOR ATTEMPTS TO LEAD, LOVE OR ENTERTAIN

+ CUNNING		
+ DARING		
+ EMPATHY		
+ MIGHT		
+ REASON		

REASON
USED FOR ACTIONS THAT USE THE MIND OR THE SENSES

+ CUNNING		
+ DARING		
+ EMPATHY		
+ MIGHT		
+ PASSION		

STRESS AND AFFLICTIONS

CONFUSION — EFFECTS: EMPATHY & REASON
STRESS CONFUSION:

AFFLICTION MADNESS:

FEAR — EFFECTS: DARING & PASSION
STRESS FEAR:

AFFLICTION TRAUMA:

INJURY — EFFECTS: CUNNING & MIGHT
STRESS INJURY:

AFFLICTION WOUNDS:

LUCK

RENOWN

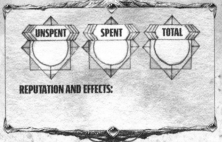

UNSPENT　SPENT　TOTAL

REPUTATION AND EFFECTS:

EXPERIENCE

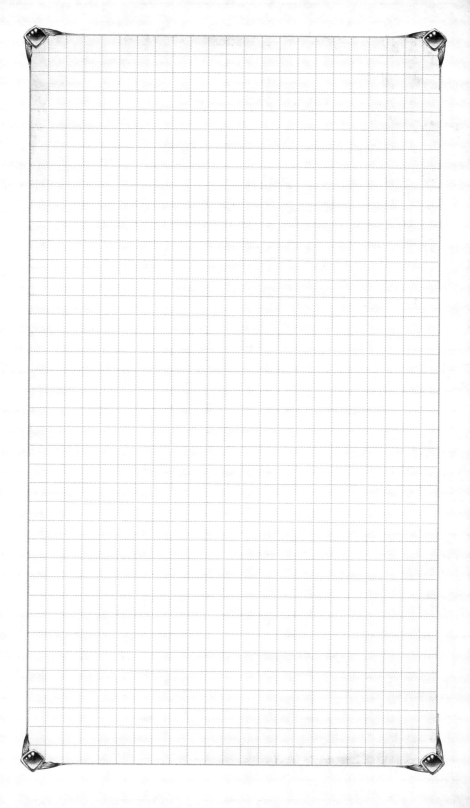

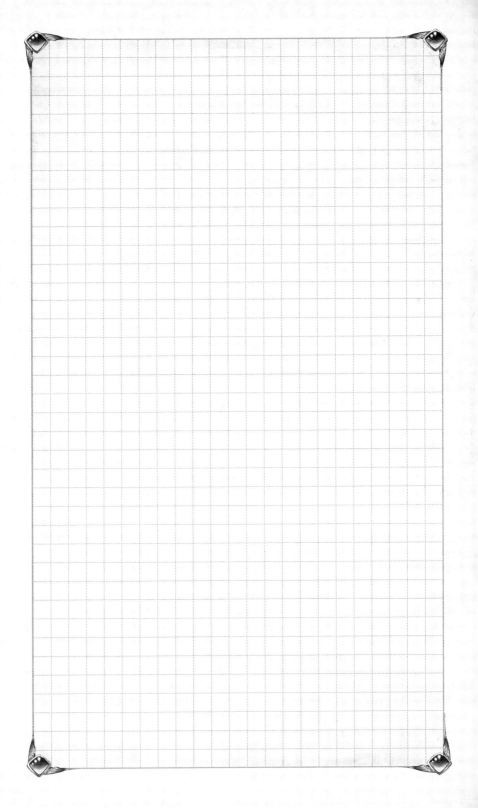

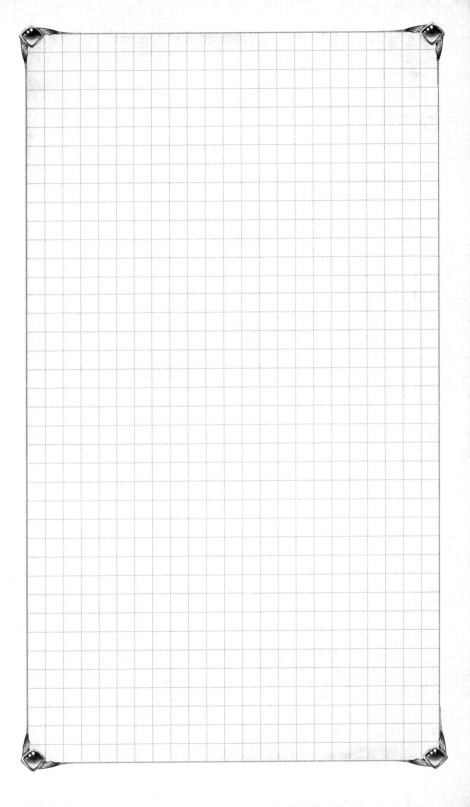